HAL•LEONARD

ro vocal®
BETTER THAN KARAOKE!

WOMEN'S EDITION

R&B
Super Hits

ISBN 0-634-07941-7

HAL•LEONARD®
CORPORATION
7777 W. BLUEMOUND RD. P.O. BOX 13819 MILWAUKEE, WI 53213

Visit Hal Leonard Online at
www.halleonard.com

Contents

PAGE	TITLE	DEMO TRACK	SING-ALONG TRACK
4	**BABY LOVE** **The Supremes**	1	9
8	**DANCING IN THE STREET** **Martha & The Vandellas**	2	10
12	**I'M SO EXCITED** **Pointer Sisters**	3	11
22	**LADY MARMALADE** **Patty LaBelle**	4	12
17	**MIDNIGHT TRAIN TO GEORGIA** **Gladys Knight & The Pips**	5	13
28	**RESCUE ME** **Fontella Bass**	6	14
32	**RESPECT** **Aretha Franklin**	7	15
36	**WHAT'S LOVE GOT TO DO WITH IT** **Tina Turner**	8	16

Baby Love

Words and Music by Brian Holland, Edward Holland and Lamont Dozier

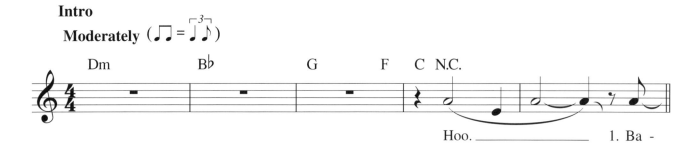

Hoo. _____ 1. Ba-

Verse

- by love, _____ my ba - by love, _____ I need _____ ya, oh, how _____ I _____

_____ need _ ya. _____ But all ya do is treat me bad, _____

break my heart and leave _____ me sad. _____ Tell me, what did I _____

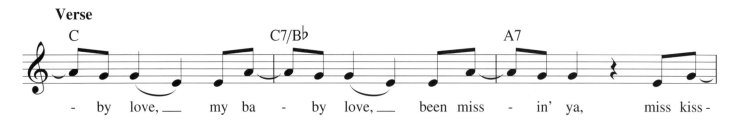

_____ do wrong _____ to make you stay _____ a - way so long? _ 2. 'Cause ba-

Verse

- by love, _____ my ba - by love, _____ been miss - in' ya, miss kiss-

- in' ya.   In - stead of break - in' up, _____

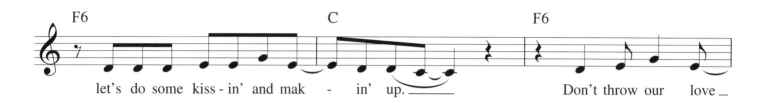

let's do some kiss-in' and mak - in' up. _____   Don't throw our   love _

_____ a - way. _____   In   my   arms, why _____ don't you   stay? ____   Need _

Interlude

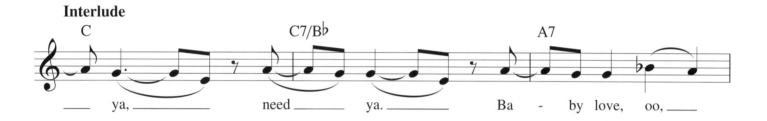

_____ ya, _____   need _____ ya. _____   Ba - by love, oo, _____

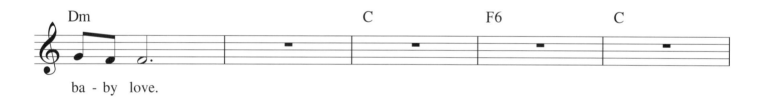

ba - by love.

3. Ba -

Verse

- by love, _____   my ba - by love, _____ why must ___ we   sep - a -

rate, my   love? _   All of my whole ___ life   through, _

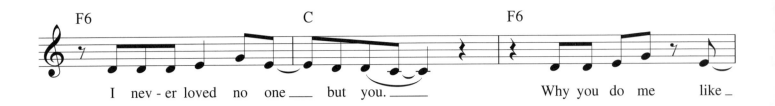

I nev - er loved no one ___ but you. ___ Why you do me like ___

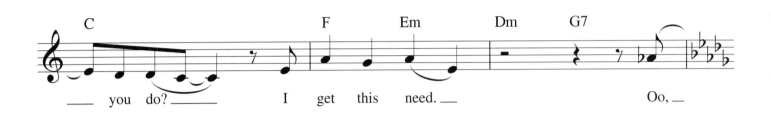

___ you do? ___ I get this need. ___ Oo, ___

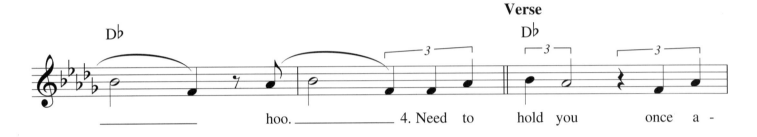

Verse

___ hoo. ___ 4. Need to hold you once a -

gain my love, feel your warm ___ em - brace, ___ my love. ___

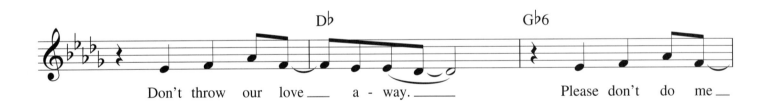

Don't throw our love ___ a - way. ___ Please don't do me ___

___ this way. ___ Not hap - py like I used to be.

Verse

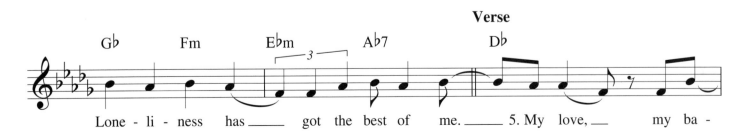

Lone - li - ness has ___ got the best of me. ___ 5. My love, ___ my ba -

Db/Cb ... Bb7 ... Ebm

- by love, ____ I need __ ya, oh, how _ I ____ need __ ya. __

Db ... Gb6

Why you do me like __ you do _____ af - ter I've been true _

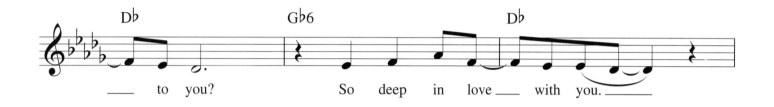

Db ... Gb6 ... Db

__ to you? So deep in love __ with you. _____

Gb ... Fm ... Ebm ... Ab7

Ba - by, ba - by. Oo, _____ 'til it's

Outro

Db ... Db7/Cb ... Bb7

hurt - in' me, 'til it's hurt - in' me. __ Oo, _____ ba -

Ebm ... Db

- by love. Don't throw our love ___ a - way.

Begin fade ... ***Fade out***

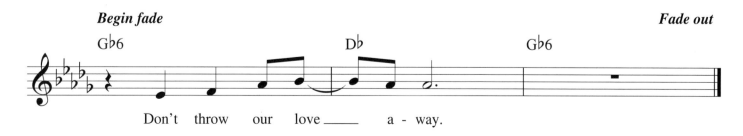

Gb6 ... Db ... Gb6

Don't throw our love ___ a - way.

Dancing in the Street

Words and Music by Marvin Gaye, Ivy Hunter and William Stevenson

Intro
Moderately

1. Call-

Verse

- ing out __ a - round __ the world, __ are you read-y for a brand new beat? __

____ Sum-mer's here __ and the time is right __ for

danc - in' __ in the street. __ They're danc - in' in Chi - ca - go, __

down in New Or - leans, __ in New York __ Cit -

y. All __ we need __ is mu - sic, sweet __ mu -

- sic. There'll _ be mu - sic ev - 'ry - where. _ There'll be

swing - in', sway - in' and rec-ords play - in', danc - in', a, in the street, _

Chorus

G#7

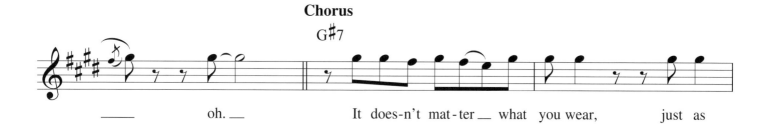

_____ oh. _ It does-n't mat-ter _ what you wear, just as

C#m

F#m

long _ as you are there. ____ So come on, ev - 'ry guy _

B7sus4   B7

grab a girl. _ Ev - 'ry - where _ a - round _ the world _ they'll be

E7

danc - in'. _ They're danc - in' in the street. ___

Verse

E7

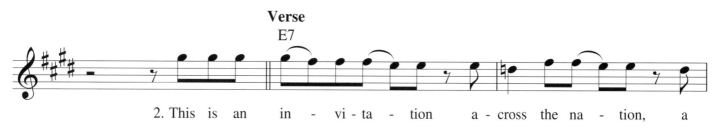

2. This is an in - vi - ta - tion a - cross the na - tion, a

chance for _ folks to meet. ___ They'll be laugh - in', sing - in' and

mu - sic swing - in', danc - in', a, in the street. ___ Phil - a - del - phia, P. A., _

___ Bal - ti - more and D. C., _ now. _

Can't for - get the Mo - tor Cit - y. All ___ we need ___ is mu -

A

- sic, sweet _ mu - sic. There'll _ be mu - sic ev - 'ry - where. _

E7

___ There'll be swing - in', sway - in' and rec - ords play - in',

Chorus

G#7

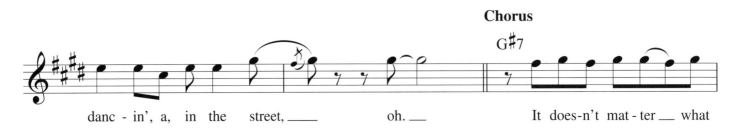

danc - in', a, in the street, ___ oh. _ It does - n't mat - ter _ what

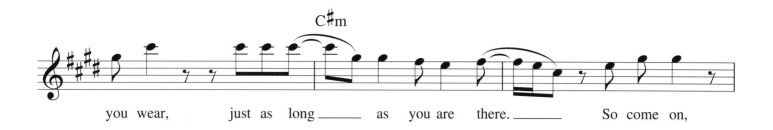

you wear,   just as long _____ as you are there. _____   So come on,

ev - 'ry guy __   grab a girl. __   Ev - 'ry - where __   a - round __

Outro

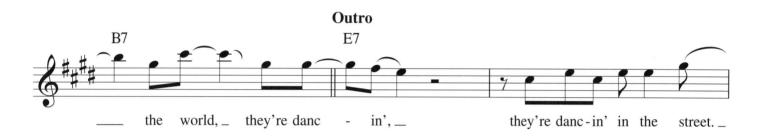

_____ the world, __ they're danc - in', __   they're danc - in' in the   street. __

_____ they're danc - in' in the   street. __   Way down in L. __   A., _____   ev - er - y day, __

_____ they're danc - in' in the   street. __   Let's form a big   strong __ line, __

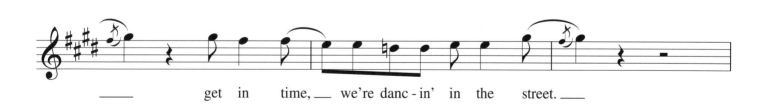

_____   get in   time, __ we're danc - in' in the   street. ___

Begin fade   *Fade out*

A-cross the o - cean __ blue, _____   me and   you, __ we're danc - in' in the   street. __

11

I'm So Excited

Words and Music by Trevor Lawrence, June Pointer, Ruth Pointer and Anita Pointer

Intro
Moderately

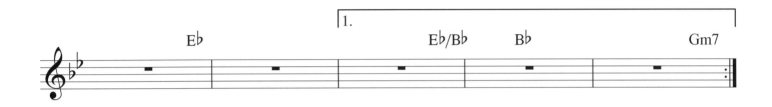

1. To - night's

Verse

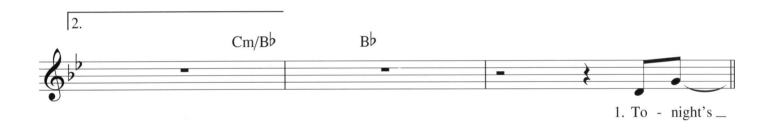

the night we're gon - na make it hap - pen,

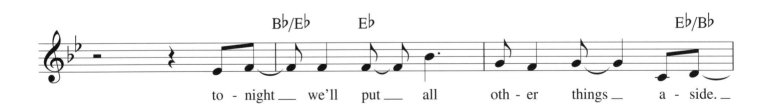

to - night we'll put all oth - er things a - side.

Give in this time and

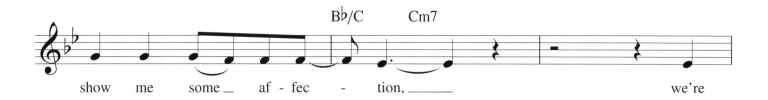

show me some af - fec - tion, _____ we're

go - in' for ___ those pleas - ures in the night. ___

𝄋 Pre-Chorus

I want to love you, feel you,

wrap my - self a - round ___ you. I want to squeeze you,

please you, I just can't get ___ e - nough. ___ And if ___ you

To Coda ⊕

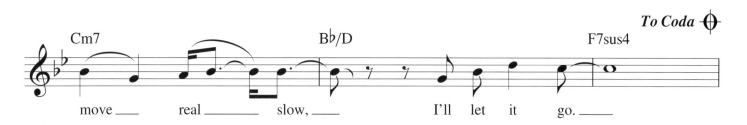

move ___ real _____ slow, ___ I'll let it go. ___

Chorus

I'm so ex - cit - ed, and I just ___ can't hide ___ it.

I'm a - bout to lose con - trol ___ and I think I like ___

Gm

___ it. I'm so ___ ex - cit - ed,

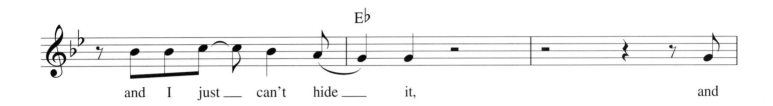

Eb

and I just ___ can't hide ___ it, and

F   Gm

I know, I know, I know, ___ I know, I know I want you.

Verse

Gm

2. We should-n't e - ven think ___ a - bout ___ to - mor -

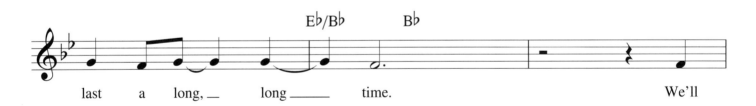

Bb/C   Cm7   Bb/Eb   Eb

- row, _____ sweet mem - o - ries ___ will ___

Eb/Bb   Bb

last a long, ___ long _____ time. We'll

Gm7   Bb/C   Cm7

have a good ___ time, ___ ba - by, don't ___ you ___ wor - ry.

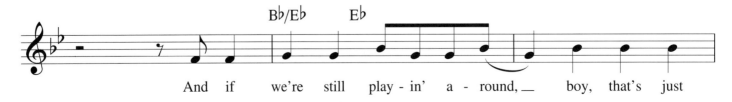

Bb/Eb   Eb

And if we're still play - in' a - round, ___ boy, that's just

Chorus

fine. Let's get ex - cit - ed. Oh,

we just ___ can't hide ___ it. No, ___ no, no. ___

I'm a - bout to lose con - trol ___ and I think I like ___ it!

I'm so ___ ex - cit - ed, and I just ___ can't hide ___

___ it. No, no. ___ And I know, I know, I know, ___

___ I know, I know I want you, I want you.

Piano Solo

Oo. ___

1.

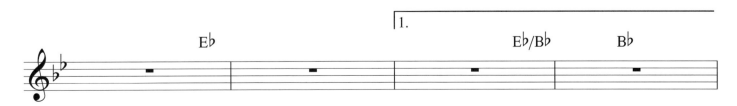

Gm7   Cm/B♭ B♭

Oo, boy, I want to

⊕ Coda

Outro-Chorus
w/ Voc. ad lib., on repeats

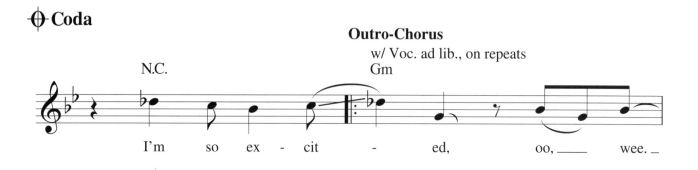

N.C.   Gm

I'm so ex - cit - ed,   oo, wee.

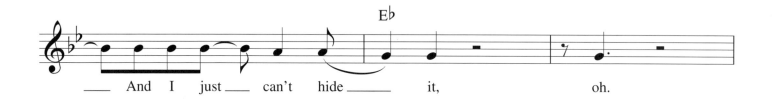

E♭

 And I just can't hide it,   oh.

F   Gm

I'm a - bout to lose con - trol and I think I like it. Oh, yeah.

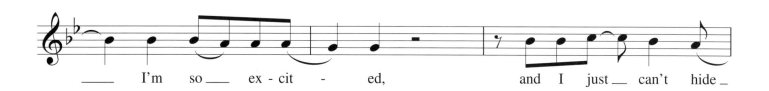

 I'm so ex - cit - ed, and I just can't hide

E♭

 it. No, no, no, no, no.   I know, I know, I know,

Repeat and fade

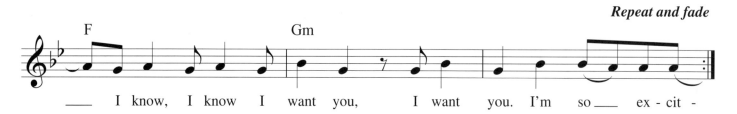

F   Gm

 I know, I know I want you, I want you. I'm so ex - cit -

Midnight Train to Georgia

Words and Music by Jim Weatherly

Intro
Moderately slow

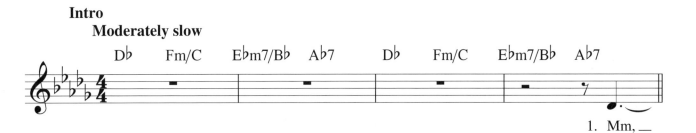

1. Mm, —

Verse

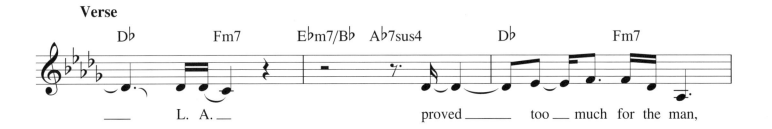

__ L. A. __ proved _____ too __ much for the man,

so he's leav-in' the life, mm, he's _

__ come to know. _____ Oo, _____ hoo, _____ hoo.

He said he's go-in' back __ to find,

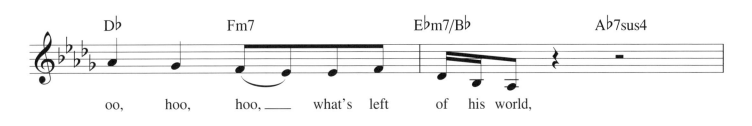

oo, hoo, hoo, ___ what's left of his world,

Chorus

18

_____ once _ knew. Oh, yes, __ he did. He said he would, ah, ha. ___

Chorus

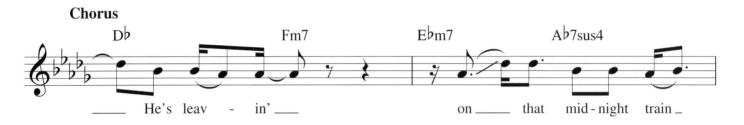

_____ He's leav - in' ___ on _____ that mid - night train _

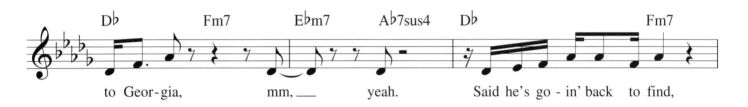

to Geor - gia, mm, ___ yeah. Said he's go - in' back to find,

oo, ___ a sim - pler place _____ and time, oo,

yeah. I'm gon - na be with him _____

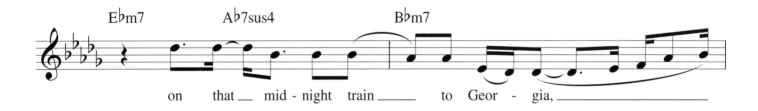

on that __ mid - night train _____ to Geor - gia, _____

oo. ___ I'd rath - er live _ in his world

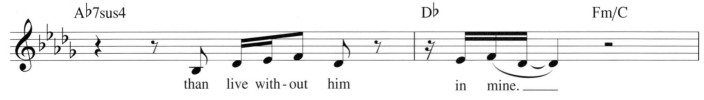

than live with - out him in mine. ___

Lady Marmalade

Words and Music by Bob Crewe and Kenny Nolan

Intro
Moderately

(Hey sis - ter, go sis - ter, soul sis - ter, go sis - ter. Hey sis - ter, go sis - ter,

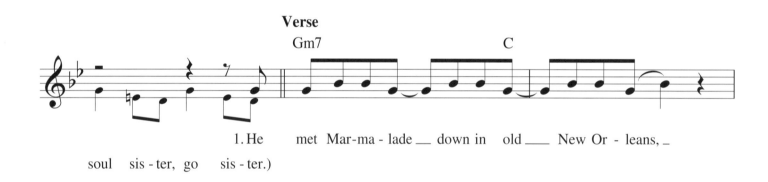

soul sis - ter, go sis - ter.)   1.He met Mar-ma - lade __ down in old __ New Or - leans, __

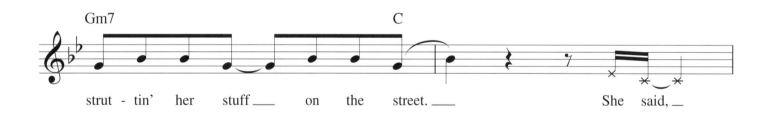

strut - tin' her stuff __ on the street. __   She said, __

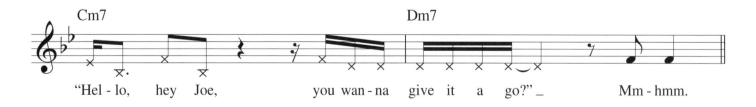

"Hel - lo, hey Joe, you wan - na give it a go?" __   Mm - hmm.

Chorus

Git - chie, git - chie, ya, ya, da, _____ da.

Git - chie, git - chie, ya, ya, here. _____

Mo - cha choc - o - la - ta, ya, _____ ya.

Cre - ole La - dy Mar - ma - lade. _____

Vou - lez vous cou - cher av - ec moi _____ ce - soir? _____

Vou - lez vous cou - cher av - ec moi? _____

Verse

2. Stayed in her bou - doir while she _____ fresh - ened up, _____

the boy ___ drank all that mag - no - lia wine. On her

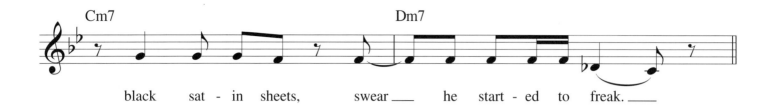

black sat - in sheets, swear ___ he start - ed to freak. ___

Chorus

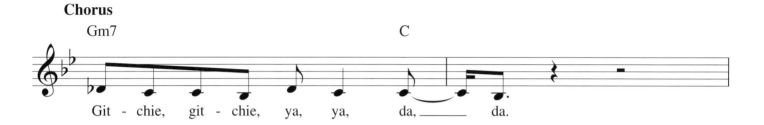

Git - chie, git - chie, ya, ya, da, ___ da.

Git - chie, git - chie, ya, ya, here. ___

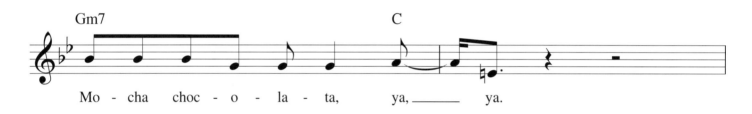

Mo - cha choc - o - la - ta, ya, ___ ya.

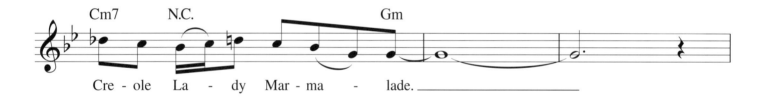

Cre - ole La - dy Mar - ma - lade. ___

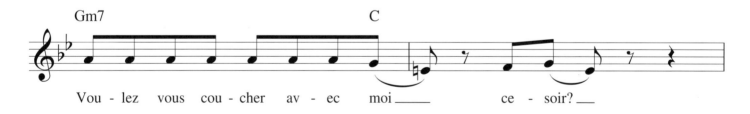

Vou - lez vous cou - cher av - ec moi ___ ce - soir? ___

Vou - lez vous cou - cher av - ec moi? ___

Interlude

Chorus

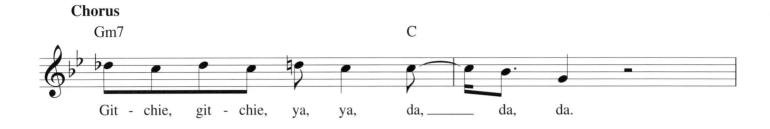

Git - chie, git - chie, ya, ya, da, ____ da, da.

Git - chie, git - chie, ya, ya, here. ____

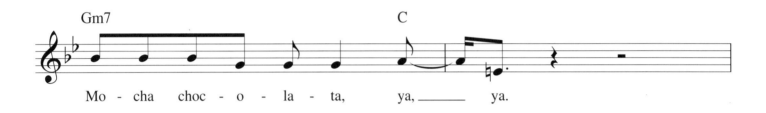

Mo - cha choc - o - la - ta, ya, ____ ya.

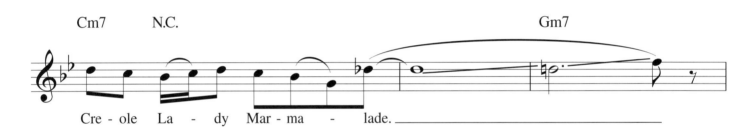

Cre - ole La - dy Mar - ma - lade. ____

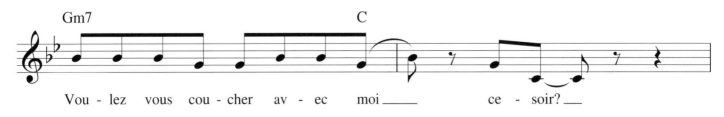

Vou - lez vous cou - cher av - ec moi ____ ce - soir? ___

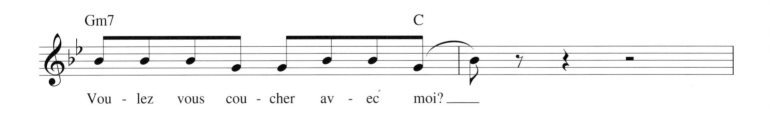

Vou - lez vous cou - cher av - ec moi? ____

Vou - lez vous cou - cher av - ec moi ____ ce - soir? ___

Cm7 N.C. Gm7

Cre-ole La - dy Mar-ma - lade.

Outro-Chorus

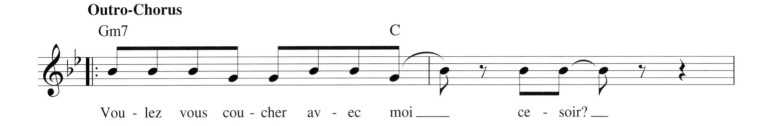

Gm7 C

Vou - lez vous cou - cher av - ec moi _____ ce - soir? _____

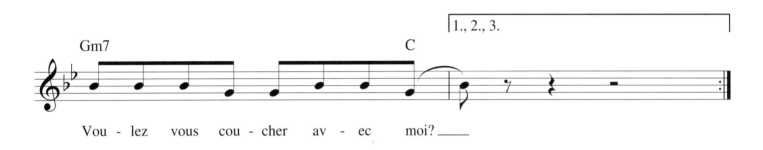

1., 2., 3.

Gm7 C

Vou - lez vous cou - cher av - ec moi? _____

4.

Gm7 C

_____ Mm - hmm. Git-chie, git-chie, ya, ya, da, _____ da.

Gm7 C

Git - chie, git - chie, ya, ya, here. _____

Begin fade

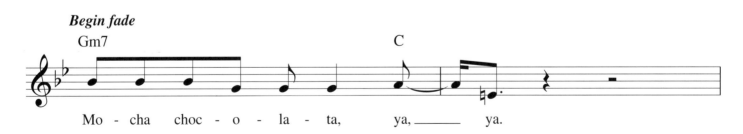

Gm7 C

Mo - cha choc - o - la - ta, ya, _____ ya.

Fade out

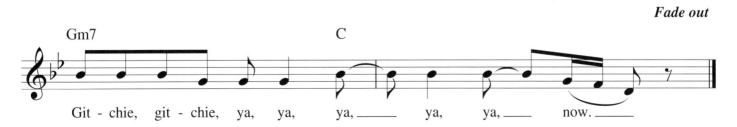

Gm7 C

Git - chie, git - chie, ya, ya, ya, _____ ya, ya, _____ now. _____

Rescue Me

Words and Music by R. Miner and C. Smith

Intro

Moderately

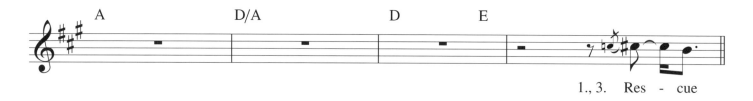

1., 3. Res - cue

Verse

me. _____ Oh, take me in your arms. _____ Res - cue _____

me. _____ I want your ten - der _____ charms, _____ 'cause I'm _____

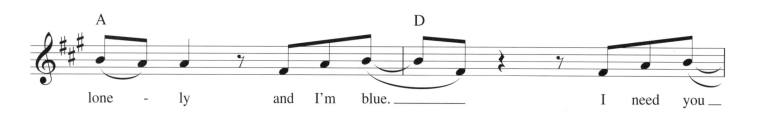

lone - ly and I'm blue. _____ I need you _____

To Coda ⊕

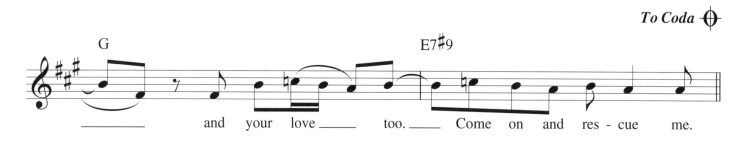

_____ and your love _____ too. _____ Come on and res - cue me.

Chorus

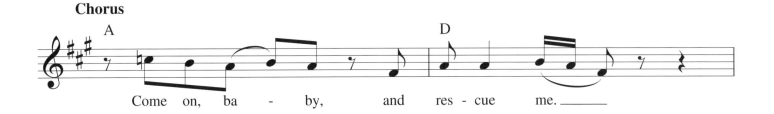

Come on, ba - by, and res - cue me. _____

Come on, ba - by, and res - cue me. _____

'Cause I need ___ you ___ by my side. _____

Verse

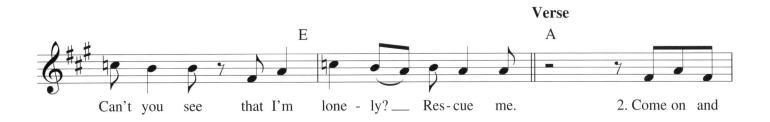

Can't you see that I'm lone - ly? __ Res - cue me. 2. Come on and

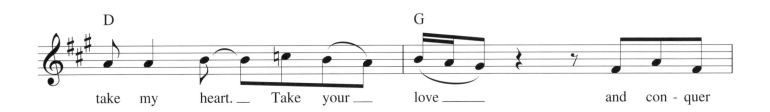

take my heart. __ Take your __ love _____ and con - quer

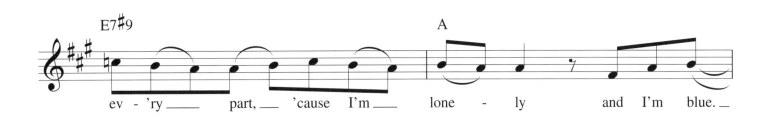

ev - 'ry ___ part, __ 'cause I'm __ lone - ly and I'm blue. __

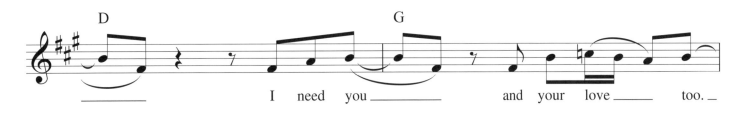

_____ I need you _____ and your love _____ too. __

Chorus

Come on and res - cue me. Come on, ba - by, and res - cue me.

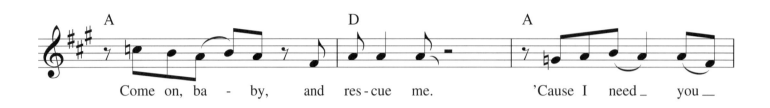

Come on, ba - by, and res - cue me. 'Cause I need you

D.C. al Coda

by my side. Can't you see that I'm lone - ly?

Coda

Bridge

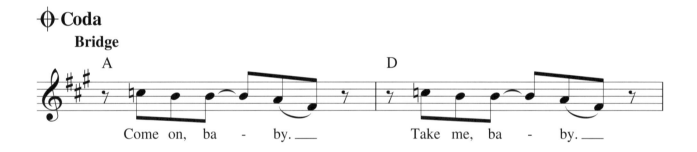

Come on, ba - by. Take me, ba - by.

Hold me, ba - by. Love me, ba - by.

Can you see that I need you, ba - by?

Verse

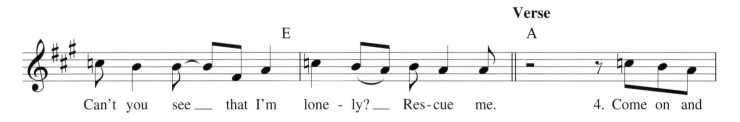

Can't you see that I'm lone - ly? Res - cue me. 4. Come on and

take my hand. ___ Come on, ba - by, and be my man. ___

'Cause I love ___ you, ___ 'cause I want ___ you. ___ Can't you see that I'm

Outro

lone - ly? ___ Mm, ___ hmm. _____ Mm, hmm. _____ Take me, ba -

- by Love me, ba - by. Need me, ba - by. Mm, hmm. _

_____ Mm, hmm. Can't you see that I'm lone - ly? ___ Res - cue

me. ___ Res - cue me. ___ Mm, _____ hmm. _ Mm, hmm. _

Begin fade   *Fade out*

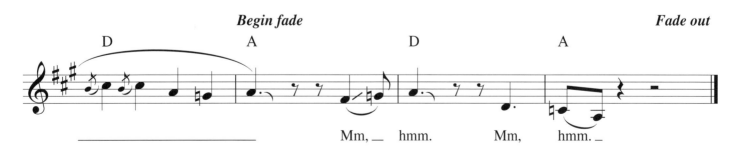

_____ Mm, _ hmm. Mm, _ hmm. _

Respect

Words and Music by Otis Redding

Intro
Moderately

Verse

1. What you __ want, ba - by, I got it.
(Hoo.)

What you __ need, __ do you know I got it?
(Hoo.)

All I'm ask - ing is for a lit - tle re -
(Hoo.)

spect when you come home. Hey, ba - by. When you come home,
(Just a lit - tle bit.) (Just a lit - tle bit.)

mis - ter.
(Just a lit - tle bit.) (Just a lit - tle bit.)

is   to   give   me___   my   prop - ers   when you get

home.   Yeah,   ba - by,   when   you   get

(Just   a,   just   a,   just   a,   just   a,   just   a,   just   a,   just   a,   just   a,

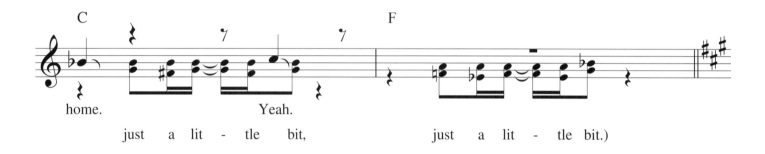

home.   Yeah.

just   a   lit - tle   bit,   just   a   lit - tle   bit.)

Sax Solo

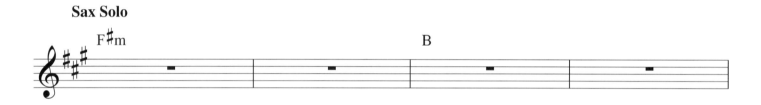

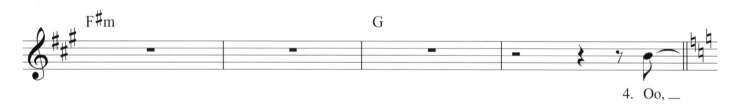

4. Oo, ___

Verse

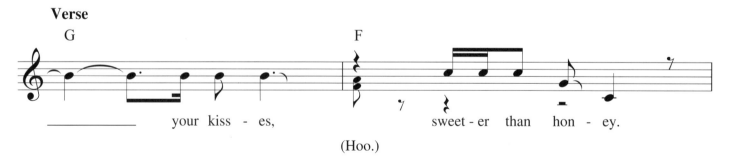

_____   your   kiss - es,   sweet - er   than   hon - ey.

(Hoo.)

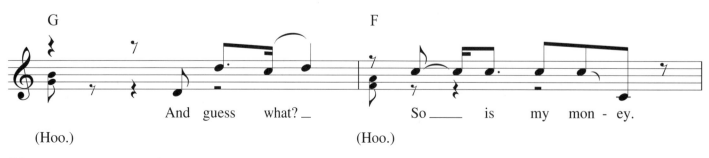

And   guess   what?___   So ___ is   my   mon - ey.

(Hoo.)   (Hoo.)

All I want you to do for __ me is give it to me
(Hoo.)   (Hoo.)

when you get home.   Hey, __ ba - by,   whip it to me
(Re -   re   re   re   re   re   re - re -

when you get   home,   yeah. __   just a lit - tle bit.)
spect.   Just   a   lit - tle bit,

Bridge

R - E - S - P - E -   C - T,   find out what it means __ to me.

R - E - S - P - E -   C - T,   take care of T. - C. - B.

Outro
2nd time, w/ Voc. ad lib., till fade

Whoa,   lit - tle re -
(Sock it to me, sock it to me, sock it to me, sock it to me.

Repeat and fade

spect.
Sock it to me, sock it to me, sock it to me, sock it to me.)

What's Love Got to Do With It

Words and Music by Terry Britten and Graham Lyle

Intro
Moderately slow

1. You

Verse

must un - der - stand, __ though the touch of __ your hand makes my

2. *See additional lyrics*

pulse re - act, __ that it's on - ly __ the thrill __ of

boy meet - ing girl; __ op - po - sites at - tract. __ It's

phys - i - cal, __ on - ly log - i - cal. __

You must try to __ ig - nore __ that it

Chorus

means   more ___   than   that.   Oh, _____   what's   love ___   got   to   do, ___

___   got   to   do ___   with   it?   What's   love ___   but   a

sec - ond - hand   e - mo - tion? ___   What's   love ___   got   to   do, ___

___   got   to   do ___   with   it?   Who   needs ___   a   heart   when ___   a

1.   heart   can ___   be   bro - ken?   2. It

2.   heart   can ___   be   bro - ken? ___

Interlude

Hoo, _____   oo. _____

Bridge

I've   been   tak - ing   on   a   new   di - rec - tion, _____

37

but I have _____ to say _____

I been think - in' a - bout my own pro - tec - tion. It

scares me to feel this way. _____ Ho, _____

Outro-Chorus
w/ Voc. ad lib., till fade

_____ what's love _____ got to do, _____ got to do _____ with it?

What's love _____ but a sec - ond - hand e - mo - tion? _

What's love _____ got to do, _____ got to do _____ with it?

Repeat and fade

Who needs _____ a heart when _____ a heart can _____ be...

Additional Lyrics

2. It may seem to you that I'm acting confused
   When you're close to me.
   If I tend to look dazed, I read it some place,
   I got cause to be.
   And there's a name for it, there's a phrase that fits.
   But whatever the reason you do it for me...

pro vocal

BETTER THAN KARAOKE!

Pro Vocal Series
SONGBOOK & SOUND-ALIKE CD
SING 8 CHART-TOPPING SONGS WITH A PROFESSIONAL BAND

Whether you're a karaoke singer or an auditioning professional, the Pro Vocal series is for you. The book contains the lyrics, melody, and chord symbols for eight hit songs. The CD contains demos for listening, and separate backing tracks so you can sing along. The CD is playable on any CD player, but it is also enhanced for PC and Mac computer users so you can adjust the recording to any pitch *without changing the tempo!* Perfect for home rehearsal, parties, auditions, corporate events, and gigs without a backup band.

Broadway Songs: Women's Edition
8 stage favorites, including: A Change in Me • I Can Hear the Bells • I'd Give My Life for You • Memory • On My Own • Someone like You • There Are Worse Things I Could Do • Without You.
_____00740247 Book/CD Pack...$12.95

Broadway Songs: Men's Edition
8 stage favorites, including: Alone at the Drive-In Movie • Any Dream Will Do • Bring Him Home • Elaborate Lives • Seasons of Love • They Live in You • This Is the Moment • Why God Why?
_____00740248 Book/CD Pack...$12.95

Christmas Standards: Women's Edition
8 holiday favorites, including: Frosty the Snow Man • Let It Snow! Let It Snow! Let It Snow! • Merry Christmas, Darling • My Favorite Things • Rockin' Around the Christmas Tree • Rudolph the Red-Nosed Reindeer • Santa Baby • Santa Claus Is Comin' to Town.
_____00740299 Book/CD Pack...$12.95

Christmas Standards: Men's Edition
8 holiday favorites, including: Blue Christmas • The Christmas Song (Chestnuts Roasting on an Open Fire) • The Christmas Waltz • Here Comes Santa Claus (Right down Santa Claus Lane) • (There's No Place Like) Home for the Holidays • I'll Be Home for Christmas • Let It Snow! Let It Snow! Let It Snow! • Silver Bells.
_____00740298 Book/CD Pack...$12.95

Contemporary Hits: Women's Edition
8 of today's top hits, including: Beautiful • Breathe • Complicated • Don't Know Why • Fallin' • The Game of Love • I Hope You Dance • My Heart Will Go On.
_____00740246 Book/CD Pack...$12.95

Contemporary Hits: Men's Edition
8 of today's top hits, including: Drive • Drops of Jupiter (Tell Me) • Fly Away • Hanging by a Moment • Iris • Smooth • 3 AM • Wherever You Will Go.
_____00740251 Book/CD Pack...$12.95

Disco Fever : Women's Edition
8 dance favorites, including: Boogie Oogie Oogie • Funkytown • Hot Stuff • I Will Survive • It's Raining Men • Le Freak • Turn the Beat Around • We Are Family.
_____00740281 Book/CD Pack...$12.95

Disco Fever: Men's Edition
8 dance favorites, including: Boogie Fever • Do Ya Think I'm Sexy • Get Down Tonight • Love Rollercoaster • Stayin' Alive • Super Freak • That's The Way (I Like It) • Y.M.C.A.
_____00740282 Book/CD Pack...$12.95

'80s Gold: Women's Edition
8 favorites from the 80s, including: Call Me • Flashdance...What a Feeling • Girls Just Want to Have Fun • How Will I Know • Material Girl • Mickey • Straight Up • Walking on Sunshine.
_____00740277 Book/CD Pack...$12.95

'80s Gold: Men's Edition
8 favorites from the 80s, including: Every Breath You Take • Heart and Soul • Hurts So Good • It's Still Rock and Roll to Me • Jessie's Girl • Maneater • Summer of '69 • You Give Love a Bad Name.
_____00740278 Book/CD Pack...$12.95

Jazz Standards: Women's Edition
8 jazz classics, including: Bye, Bye Blackbird • Come Rain or Come Shine • Fever • The Girl from Ipanema (Garôta De Ipanema) • Lullaby of Birdland • My Funny Valentine • Stormy Weather (Keeps Rainin' All the Time) • Tenderly.
_____00740249 Book/CD Pack...$12.95

Jazz Standards: Men's Edition
8 jazz classics, including: Ain't Misbehavin' • Don't Get Around Much Anymore • Fly Me to the Moon (In Other Words) • Georgia on My Mind • I've Got You Under My Skin • Misty • My One and Only Love • Route 66.
_____00740250 Book/CD Pack...$12.95

R&B Super Hits: Women's Edition
8 classic R&B standards: Baby Love • Dancing in the Street • I'm So Excited • Lady Marmalade • Midnight Train to Georgia • Rescue Me • Respect • What's Love Got to Do with It.
_____00740279 Book/CD Pack...$12.95

R&B Super Hits: Men's Edition
8 classic R&B standards: Brick House • I Can't Help Myself (Sugar Pie, Honey Bunch) • I Got You (I Feel Good) • In the Midnight Hour • Let's Get It On • My Girl • Shining Star • Superstition.
_____00740280 Book/CD Pack...$12.95